긍정 확언
영어 필기체 쓰기

긍정 확언 영어 필기체 쓰기

지은이 퍼포먼스 코치 리아 (Leah Jean Kim)
펴낸이 임상진
펴낸곳 (주)넥서스

초판 1쇄 발행 2023년 12월 10일
초판 2쇄 발행 2023년 12월 15일

출판신고 1992년 4월 3일 제311-2002-2호
주소 10880 경기도 파주시 지목로 5
전화 (02)330-5500 팩스 (02)330-5555

ISBN 979-11-6683-665-7 13740

www.nexusbook.com

긍정 확언
영어 필기체 쓰기

퍼포먼스 코치 리아 지음
Leah Jean Kim

넥서스

원어민 MP3 듣는 법

❶ 스마트폰에서 MP3 바로 듣기

MP3

스마트폰으로 QR코드를 인식하면
MP3를 바로 들을 수 있습니다.

❷ 컴퓨터에서 MP3 다운받기

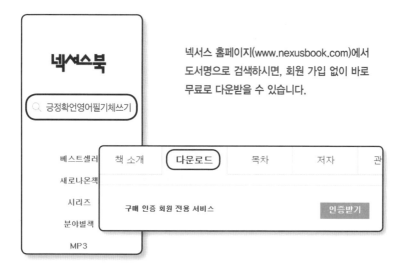

넥서스 홈페이지(www.nexusbook.com)에서
도서명으로 검색하시면, 회원 가입 없이 바로
무료로 다운받을 수 있습니다.

목차

Capital Letters

필기체 대문자

$\mathcal{A}$
A

$\mathcal{B}$
B

$\mathcal{C}$
C

$\mathcal{D}$
D

$\mathcal{E}$
E

$\mathcal{F}$
F

$\mathcal{G}$
G

$\mathcal{H}$
H

$\mathcal{I}$
I

$\mathcal{J}$
J

$\mathcal{K}$
K

$\mathcal{L}$
L

$\mathcal{M}$
M

$\mathcal{N}$
N

$\mathcal{O}$
O

$\mathcal{P}$
P

$\mathcal{Q}$
Q

$\mathcal{R}$
R

$\mathcal{S}$
S

$\mathcal{T}$
T

$\mathcal{U}$
U

$\mathcal{V}$
V

$\mathcal{W}$
W

$\mathcal{X}$
X

$\mathcal{Y}$
Y

$\mathcal{Z}$
Z

Small Letters

a

b

c

d

e

f

g

h

i

j

k

l

m

n

o

p

q

r

s

t

u

v

w

x

y

z

Writing Alphabet

A a

ag와 ar을 써보세요.

a a a
a a a
ag ag ag
ar ar ar

B b

be와 by를 써보세요.

B B B
b b b
be be be
by by by

C c

ca와 ch를 써보세요.

C C C
c c c
ca ca ca
ch ch ch

D d

de와 do를 써보세요.

D D D
d d d
de de de
do do do

E e

ed와 ev를 써보세요.

E E E
e e e
ed ed ed
ev ev ev

F f

F F F

f f f

fa와 fr을 써보세요.

fa fa fa

fr fr fr

G g

G G G

g g g

ga와 gr을 써보세요.

ga ga ga

gr gr gr

H h

H H H

h h h

ho와 hy를 써보세요.

ho ho ho

hy hy hy

I i

I I I

i i i

il과 in을 써보세요.

il il il

in in in

J j

J J J

j j j

je와 jo를 써보세요.

je je je

jo jo jo

Writing Alphabet

ke와 ky를 써보세요.

K K K

k k k

ke ke ke

ky ky ky

la와 lu를 써보세요.

L L L

l l l

la la la

lu lu lu

mo와 mu를 써보세요.

M M M

m m m

mo mo mo

mu mu mu

ne와 ny를 써보세요.

N N N

n n n

ne ne ne

ny ny ny

on과 oo를 써보세요.

O O O

o o o

on on on

oo oo oo

P P P

P p p

pa와 pr을 써보세요.

pa pa pa

pr pr pr

Q Q Q

q q q

qu와 qi를 써보세요.

qu qu qu

qi qi qi

R R R

r r r

rr과 ry를 써보세요.

rr rr rr

ry ry ry

S S S

s s s

se와 so를 써보세요.

se se se

so so so

T T T

t t t

th와 to를 써보세요.

th th th

to to to

Writing Alphabet

U U U

U u

u u u

un과 us를 써보세요.

un un un

us us us

V V V

V v

v v v

vi와 vy를 써보세요.

vi vi vi

vy vy vy

W W W

W w

w w w

wa와 wh를 써보세요.

wa wa wa

wh wh wh

X X X

X x

x x x

xe와 xy를 써보세요.

xe xe xe

xy xy xy

Y Y Y

Y y

y y y

ye와 yo를 써보세요.

ye ye ye

yo yo yo

ze와 zo를 써보세요.

Z Z Z

ze ze ze

Z Z Z

zo zo zo

Z z

대문자 이어 써보기

ABCDEFGHIJKLMNOPQRSTUVWXYZ

소문자 이어 써보기

abcdefghijklmnopqrstuvwxyz

이 책의 활용법

✦ 〈긍정 확언 영어 필기체 쓰기〉는 퍼포먼스 코치 리아의 〈하루 한 장 영어 일력 365〉에 수록
된 문장들 중 엄선하여 필기체로 쓸 수 있도록 만든 책입니다. 12개의 테마로 이루어진 다양한
긍정 확언을 써 보며 새로운 영감을 얻는 동시에 영어 필기체 쓰기 연습도 해 보세요.

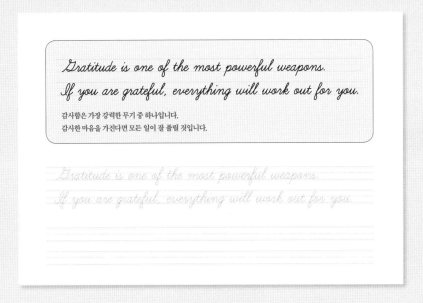

✦ 저자 유튜브(언바운디드 영어필사)에서 더욱 다양한 콘텐츠를 만나 보실 수 있습니다.

YouTube
바로가기

영어 필기체 쓰기

Gratitude

감사

'감사'와 관련된 나를 위한 긍정 메시지를 필기체로 써 보세요.

Gratitude is one of the most powerful weapons.
If you are grateful, everything will work out for you.

감사함은 가장 강력한 무기 중 하나입니다.
감사한 마음을 가진다면 모든 일이 잘 풀릴 것입니다.

Gratitude is one of the most powerful weapons.
If you are grateful, everything will work out for you.

Can you savor all the things you already have?
If not, nothing will fully satisfy you.

당신은 당신이 이미 가지고 있는 모든 것들을 음미하고 있나요?
그렇지 않다면, 어떤 것도 당신을 완전히 만족시킬 수 없을 것입니다.

Can you savor all the things you already have?
If not, nothing will fully satisfy you.

You get to decide what you experience in life.
It can be wonderful or dreadful.

삶에서 무엇을 경험할지는 당신이 결정하는 것입니다.
멋질 수도 있고 끔찍할 수도 있습니다.

You get to decide what you experience in life.
It can be wonderful or dreadful.

There are people who love and support you.

Focus on them, not on haters.

당신을 사랑하고 응원하는 사람들이 있습니다.
당신을 싫어하는 사람들이 아닌 그들에게 집중하세요.

There are people who love and support you.

Focus on them, not on haters.

Where you are right now is someone else's dream.

Remind yourself how blessed you are.

당신의 지금 위치는 누군가의 꿈입니다.
당신이 얼마나 축복받았는지 기억하세요.

Where you are right now is someone else's dream.

Remind yourself how blessed you are.

If you ever find yourself blaming or complaining,
stop. There are zero upsides to the victim mentality.

비난이나 불평을 하고 있다면, 멈추세요.
피해 의식을 갖는 것에 이점은 없습니다.

If you ever find yourself blaming or complaining,
stop. There are zero upsides to the victim mentality

Do you want to feel abundant? Practice gratitude.
Feeling like enough is an internal game.

풍요를 느끼고 싶으신가요? 감사함을 연습하세요.
충분함을 느끼는 것은 내면에 달려 있습니다.

Do you want to feel abundant? Practice gratitude.
Feeling like enough is an internal game.

No one has a perfect life. People who look happier just have different perspectives.

완벽한 삶을 사는 사람은 없습니다.
더 행복해 보이는 사람은 단지 다른 관점을 가진 것입니다.

No one has a perfect life. People who look happier just have different perspectives.

There's no way you can feel negative and grateful at the same time. What do you choose to indulge in?

부정적인 감정과 감사함을 동시에 느낄 수 있는 방법은 없습니다.
당신은 어떤 것을 느끼길 원하나요?

There's no way you can feel negative and grateful at the same time. What do you choose to indulge in?

The grass isn't greener on the other side. There's no such place where only positive emotions exist.

다른 쪽의 잔디가 더 푸르지 않습니다. (더 나은 곳은 없습니다.)
긍정적인 감정만 있는 곳은 존재하지 않습니다.

The grass isn't greener on the other side. There's no such place where only positive emotions exist.

Being positive is not a naive attitude. It's the ability to not let anyone or anything take control of you.

긍정적인 것이 순진하다는 뜻은 아닙니다. 긍정이란 그 누구도, 어떤 것도 당신을 통제하게 내버려 두지 않는 능력입니다.

Being positive is not a naive attitude. It's the ability to not let anyone or anything take control of you.

Feel gratitude ahead of time.

Experience your future feelings now.

미리 감사함을 느껴 보세요

당신의 미래 감정(감사함)을 지금 경험하세요

Feel gratitude ahead of time.

Experience your future feelings now.

Gratitude is a clever strategy. It is a deliberate tactic to let every circumstance work for you.

감사하는 마음은 똑똑한 전략입니다. 모든 환경이 당신을 위해 일하도록 하는 의도적인 전략입니다.

Gratitude is a clever strategy. It is a deliberate tactic to let every circumstance work for you.

Want what you already own. You already have so many things that you desire deeply.

당신이 이미 가진 것들을 원하세요. 당신은 이미 당신이 깊이 갈망하는 수많은 것들을 가지고 있습니다.

Want what you already own. You already have so
many things that you desire deeply.

Gratitude is an attitude. It doesn't come naturally when things change. It's a deliberate choice.

감사는 태도입니다. 상황이 바뀌면 자연스럽게 감사한 마음이 생기지 않습니다.
감사는 의도적인 선택입니다.

Gratitude is an attitude. It doesn't come naturally
when things change. It's a deliberate choice.

Joy

즐거움

'즐거움'과 관련된 나를 위한 긍정 메시지를 필기체로 써 보세요.

What are you happy about in your life? What makes you smile? Can you stay in that joy for a moment?

당신 인생의 행복은 무엇인가요? 당신을 웃게 만드는 것은 무엇인가요?
잠시라도 그 기쁨에 머무를 수 있나요?

What are you happy about in your life? What makes
you smile? Can you stay in that joy for a moment?

Feeling entitled to be joyful all of the time may block
you from experiencing it fully.

늘 즐거울 자격이 있다고 생각하는 것은 그것(즐거움)을 충분히 경험하는 것을 막을 수 있습니다.

Feeling entitled to be joyful all of the time may block
you from experiencing it fully.

If you want more joy in your life, choose it. Look for
things to laugh, smile, and feel excited about.

당신의 인생에서 더 많은 즐거움을 원한다면 선택하세요. 당신을 웃게 하고, 미소 짓게 하고, 행복하게 만드
는 것을 찾아보세요.

If you want more joy in your life, choose it. Look for
things to laugh, smile, and feel excited about.

Your joy does not steal anyone else's joy.
Feel safe to have greater joy in your life.

당신의 즐거움은 타인의 기쁨을 빼앗는 것이 아닙니다.
당신의 삶에서 더 큰 즐거움을 가지는 것에 안심하세요.

Your joy does not steal anyone else's joy.
Feel safe to have greater joy in your life.

Imagine people are happy to see you every time you walk into a room. Assume you are loved.

여러분이 가는 곳마다 사람들이 여러분을 보고 기뻐한다고 상상해 보세요.
당신이 사랑받고 있다고 가정하세요.

Imagine people are happy to see you every time you walk into a room. Assume you are loved.

Choose joy over immediate gratifications.
Short-term pleasures might rob your long-term joy.

즉각적인 만족보다는 기쁨을 선택하세요.
단기간의 쾌락은 장기간의 기쁨을 앗아갈 수 있습니다.

Choose joy over immediate gratifications.
Short-term pleasures might rob your long-term joy.

Allowing yourself to experience joy is a form of self-care, self-trust, and self-appreciation.

여러분 자신에게 기쁨을 경험하게 하는 것은 자기 관리, 자기 신뢰, 자기 감상의 한 형태입니다.

Allowing yourself to experience joy is a form of self-care, self-trust, and self-appreciation.

If you want your life to be filled with joy,
don't set it aside like it can wait "until you get there."

당신의 삶이 기쁨으로 가득하길 바란다면 "그곳에 도착할 때까지" 기다릴 수 있는 것처럼 그것(기쁨)을 미루지 마세요.

If you want your life to be filled with joy,
don't set it aside like it can wait "until you get there."

No matter how small or big, enjoy your victory.
It will help you create more of it.

얼마나 작든 크든 간에, 여러분의 승리를 즐거워하세요.
그것은 여러분이 더 많은 것을 만들 수 있도록 도와줄 것입니다.

No matter how small or big, enjoy your victory
It will help you create more of it.

There is no upside to being cynical.
All you get from that are problems.

냉소적이 되는 것에는 좋은 점이 없습니다.
그것(냉소적이 되는 것)으로부터 얻는 것은 문제점들입니다.

There is no upside to being cynical.
All you get from that are problems.

If you are unhappy, ask yourself;
"In what ways am I blocking my own happiness?"

만약 여러분이 불행하다면, 스스로에게 물어보세요.
"나는 어떤 방식으로 나 자신의 행복을 막고 있나?"

If you are unhappy, ask yourself;
"In what ways am I blocking my own happiness?"

Train yourself to enjoy doing the hard things.
There's so much joy in growth.

힘든 일을 즐기도록 자신을 훈련시키세요.
성장에는 기쁨이 넘칩니다.

Train yourself to enjoy doing the hard things.
There's so much joy in growth.

Make plans to share a laugh with people you love.
It will bring so much happiness to your day.

여러분이 사랑하는 사람들과 웃음을 나눌 계획을 세우세요.
당신의 일상에 많은 행복을 가져다 줄 것입니다.

Make plans to share a laugh with people you love.
It will bring so much happiness to your day.

You can be sad that it's gone,

or you can smile that it happened.

어떤 것이 당신 인생에서 사라진 것에 슬퍼할 수 있습니다.
또는 그 일이 당신의 삶에서 일어났다는 것으로 웃을 수도 있습니다.

You can be sad that it's gone,

or you can smile that it happened.

Fake pleasures may damage your self-esteem while

true joy boosts your sense of self-worth.

거짓 쾌락은 당신의 자존감에 상처를 줄 수 있는 반면에 진정한 기쁨은 여러분의 자존감을 높여 줍니다.

Fake pleasures may damage your self-esteem while

true joy boosts your sense of self-worth.

Courage

용기

'용기'와 관련된 나를 위한 긍정 메시지를 필기체로 써 보세요.

Courage doesn't mean you don't feel scared at all.
Courage means you move forward nonetheless.

용기란 두려움을 전혀 느끼지 못한다는 것이 아닙니다.
용기란 그럼에도 앞으로 나아간다는 것을 말합니다.

Courage doesn't mean you don't feel scared at all.
Courage means you move forward nonetheless.

Remind yourself how brave you are. You showed up to your life, even with all of the difficulties.

당신이 얼마나 용감한지 다시 한번 생각해 보세요. 당신은 모든 어려움에도 불구하고 당신의 삶에 나타났습니다.

Remind yourself how brave you are. You showed up to your life, even with all of the difficulties.

There will always be excuses why you can't do what you want to do. Do it regardless.

왜 당신이 하고 싶은 것을 할 수 없는지에 대한 변명은 항상 있을 것입니다.
상관없이 하세요.

There will always be excuses why you can't do what you want to do. Do it regardless.

Be open to making mistakes. Once you are willing to fail, you will access your own ingenuity.

실수하는 것에 마음을 여세요. 여러분이 기꺼이 실패한다면, 여러분은 여러분 자신의 독창성을 사용할 수 있을 것입니다.

Be open to making mistakes. Once you are willing to fail, you will access your own ingenuity.

Don't give up in advance because you are afraid of failing in the future.

미래에 실패할 것이 두렵다고 미리 포기하지 마세요.

Don't give up in advance because you are afraid of failing in the future.

Give yourself permission to dream big.
Let yourself have seemingly impossible dreams.

큰 꿈을 꾸도록 스스로를 허락하세요
불가능해 보이는 꿈을 꾸도록 하세요

Give yourself permission to dream big.
Let yourself have seemingly impossible dreams.

Brave people know this to be true:
failing forward is always worth it.

용감한 사람들은 이것이 사실이라는 것을 압니다.
앞으로 실패하는 것은 항상 가치가 있습니다.

Brave people know this to be true:
failing forward is always worth it.

Don't compromise your values because you are afraid of people's judgment. Let yourself be you.

사람들의 판단이 두렵다고 여러분의 가치를 타협하지 마세요.
당신답게 행동하세요.

Don't compromise your values because you are afraid of people's judgment. Let yourself be you.

You can be the nicest person on the planet and still show the world how you can achieve amazing things.

당신은 세상에서 가장 친절한 사람이 되는 동시에 얼마나 놀라운 일을 성취해 낼 수 있는지 세상에 보여 줄 수 있습니다.

You can be the nicest person on the planet and still show the world how you can achieve amazing things.

Show me a man or woman who has achieved great
success without having experienced the pain of growth.

성장의 고통을 경험하지 않고 굉장한 성공을 거둔 사람이 있다면 보여 주세요.

Show me a man or woman who has achieved great

success without having experienced the pain of growth.

Don't wait to be fully ready.
You'll get better once you start doing it.

완전히 준비되기를 기다리지 마세요.
일단 하기 시작하면, 당신은 잘하게 될 것입니다.

Don't wait to be fully ready.

You'll get better once you start doing it.

If you were sure you were going to fail and still went all in every time, how would your life be different?

만약 당신이 실패할 것이라고 확신했지만 그래도 여전히 항상 모든 것을 걸었다면, 여러분의 삶은 어떻게 달라졌을까요?

If you were sure you were going to fail and still went all in every time, how would your life be different?

Don't be afraid of what you can't control. Be afraid of not even doing something that you can control.

당신이 통제할 수 없는 것을 두려워하지 마세요.
통제할 수 있는 것조차 어떻게 하지 않는 것을 두려워하세요.

Don't be afraid of what you can't control. Be afraid of not even doing something that you can control

The next version of yourself will create what you
desire now. Are you willing to take the next step?

당신의 다음 버전은 당신이 지금 원하는 것을 창조할 것입니다.
기꺼이 다음 단계로 가실 건가요?

The next version of yourself will create what you
desire now. Are you willing to take the next step?

We are true to ourselves when we stop running from
what we fear and step into discomfort.

우리가 두려워하는 것으로부터의 도피를 멈추고 그 불편함에 발을 들여놓을 때 우리는 우리 자신에게 충실합
니다.

We are true to ourselves when we stop running from
what we fear and step into discomfort.

Goal

목표

'목표'와 관련된 나를 위한 긍정 메시지를 필기체로 써 보세요.

Imagine a future where you've achieved all of your goals. How proud would you be?

여러분이 모든 목표를 성취한 미래를 상상해 보세요.
얼마나 자랑스러우시겠어요?

Imagine a future where you've achieved all of your goals. How proud would you be?

To achieve all of your goals, pick one goal at a time.
Do one task at a time.

여러분의 모든 목표를 달성하기 위해서, 한 번에 한 가지 목표를 선택하세요.
한 번에 하나의 작업을 수행하세요.

To achieve all of your goals, pick one goal at a time.
Do one task at a time.

Making decisions is a huge part of getting things done.
Decide what to prioritize and honor it.

결정을 내리는 것은 일을 완수하는 데 있어 큰 부분을 차지합니다.
우선순위를 정하고 이를 준수하십시오.

Making decisions is a huge part of getting things done.
Decide what to prioritize and honor it.

Take big steps to get what you truly desire. Commit to
act massively and fail massively until you get it.

여러분이 진정으로 원하는 것을 얻기 위해 큰 조치를 취하세요.
이를 달성할 때까지 엄청나게 행동하고, 실패하는 것에 전념하세요.

Take big steps to get what you truly desire. Commit to
act massively and fail massively until you get it.

If you forget your "why," think about how your life
will change once you reach your goal.

나만의 이유를 잊어버렸다면, 목표에 도달했을 때 나의 삶이 어떻게 변화할지 생각해 보세요.

If you forget your "why," think about how your life
will change once you reach your goal.

What if you knew for sure that you would succeed?
Would you give up in the process?

만약 당신이 성공할 것이라는 것을 확실히 안다면 어떨까요?
그 과정에서 포기하실 건가요?

What if you knew for sure that you would succeed?
Would you give up in the process?

Motivation is useless unless you take action.
Nothing will work unless you do.

당신이 행동을 취하지 않는 한 동기부여는 소용이 없습니다.
당신이 하지 않으면 아무것도 효과가 없습니다.

Motivation is useless unless you take action.
Nothing will work unless you do.

There are two trophies in this race. Who you become in the process, and what you get as a by-product.

이 경주에는 두 개의 트로피가 있습니다. 하나는 그 과정에서 여러분이 되는 사람이고, 다른 하나는 부산물로 여러분이 얻는 것입니다.

There are two trophies in this race. Who you become in the process, and what you get as a by-product.

"Belief" comes before "how." Know-how doesn't get you there, but believing hard will.

"어떻게"보다 "믿음"이 먼저입니다. 노하우가 당신을 그곳까지 데려다주지 못합니다.
하지만 강한 믿음은 나를 데려다줄 것입니다.

"Belief" comes before "how." Know-how doesn't get you there, but believing hard will.

Revisit all of your achievements and ask yourself:
What made these things possible in my life?

모든 성과를 다시 확인하고 스스로에게 물어보세요.
제 인생에서 이것들을 가능하게 해 준 것은 무엇이었을까요?

Revisit all of your achievements and ask yourself:
What made these things possible in my life?

What is it that you truly want?
What's holding you back from it?

당신이 진정으로 원하는 것은 무엇인가요?
무엇이 그것을 망설이게 하나요?

What is it that you truly want?
What's holding you back from it?

Choosing to be positive is great. However, choosing to be effective is the best way to reach your goals.

궁정적이 되는 것을 선택하는 것은 좋습니다.
하지만 효과적이기를 선택하는 것은 여러분의 목표에 도달하는 가장 좋은 방법입니다.

Choosing to be positive is great. However, choosing to be effective is the best way to reach your goals.

Don't underestimate how much work you need to put in to fulfill your goals.

당신의 목표를 달성하기 위해 해야 할 행동의 양을 과소평가하지 마세요.

Don't underestimate how much work you need to put in to fulfill your goals.

Humble people say that they were lucky, but the truth is, no one has ever reached their goals by simple luck.

겸손한 사람들은 운이 좋았다고 하지만 사실은 단순히 운으로 자신의 목표에 도달한 사람은 아무도 없습니다.

Humble people say that they were lucky, but the truth is, no one has ever reached their goals by simple luck.

If you are not executing your plans, your goal will only exist in your mind.

계획을 실행하지 않을 경우, 당신의 목표는 오직 마음속에만 존재할 것입니다.

If you are not executing your plans, your goal will only exist in your mind.

Becoming

되기

'되기'와 관련된 나를 위한 긍정 메시지를 필기체로 써 보세요.

Imagine how unstoppable you'd be if you could only focus on becoming the best version of yourself.

당신의 최고의 모습이 되는 데에만 집중했을 때 당신이 얼마나 무적이 될지 상상해 보세요

Imagine how unstoppable you'd be if you could only focus on becoming the best version of yourself.

The point is not to eliminate discomfort.
The point is to grow bigger than the challenges.

핵심은 불편함을 없애는 것이 아닙니다.
어려움보다 더 성장하는 것이 핵심입니다.

The point is not to eliminate discomfort.
The point is to grow bigger than the challenges.

Decide who you want to become.
Decide how you want to be remembered.

어떤 사람이 되고 싶은지 결정하세요.
어떻게 기억되고 싶은지 결정하세요.

Decide who you want to become.
Decide how you want to be remembered.

When you need wisdom, ask this question:
"What would the best version of myself do?"

지혜가 필요할 때, 이 질문을 해 보세요.
"최상의 버전의 나는 과연 어떻게 했을까?"

When you need wisdom, ask this question:
"What would the best version of myself do?"

Luck can't define your future. It's up to you to decide
how much power it will have over your life.

행운이 당신의 미래를 정의할 수 없습니다.
행운이 당신의 인생에 얼마나 작용할지는 당신에게 달려 있습니다.

Luck can't define your future. It's up to you to decide
how much power it will have over your life.

What does your future self believe about your goals?
What does your future self think about setbacks?

당신의 미래 모습은 당신의 목표에 대해 어떤 믿음을 갖고 있을까요?
당신의 미래 모습은 당신의 좌절에 대해 어떻게 생각할까요?

What does your future self believe about your goals?
What does your future self think about setbacks?

Train yourself to do hard and boring things.
You will continue to grow and expand.

어렵고 지루한 일을 하는 것을 연습하세요.
당신은 계속 성장하고 확장될 겁니다.

Train yourself to do hard and boring things.
You will continue to grow and expand.

Becoming who you want to be doesn't always feel dreamy. A lot of times, it feels overwhelming.

당신이 되고자 하는 사람이 되는 과정이 매번 멋진 기분만 드는 것은 아닙니다.
많은 경우, 위압감을 느끼게 됩니다.

Becoming who you want to be doesn't always feel
dreamy. A lot of times, it feels overwhelming.

Don't wait for something magical to happen. Take charge and make miraculous things happen for you.

마법 같은 일이 일어나길 기다리지 마세요. 주도권을 갖고 행동하고 기적이 일어나도록 하세요.

Don't wait for something magical to happen. Take
charge and make miraculous things happen for you.

Regardless of your failures in the past, you can always build the life you want with a clean slate.

과거의 실패와 상관없이, 당신은 언제나 원하는 삶을 백지에서부터 만들어갈 수 있습니다.

Regardless of your failures in the past, you can always build the life you want with a clean slate.

Put your time and energy into making the possibility a reality. Not the other way around.

가능성을 현실로 만드는 데 당신의 시간과 힘을 쏟으세요.
그 반대에 시간을 쏟지 마세요.

Put your time and energy into making the possibility a reality. Not the other way around.

Everything worthwhile is supposed to be hard.
Normalize difficulty.

가치 있는 모든 것은 어렵기 마련입니다.
그 어려움에 익숙해지세요.

Everything worthwhile is supposed to be hard.
Normalize difficulty.

Decide to drop useless, unwanted and outdated stories.
Believe in new stories that benefit you.

쓸모없고 반갑지 않은 구시대적 이야기는 버리세요.
당신에게 도움이 되는 새로운 이야기를 믿으세요.

Decide to drop useless, unwanted and outdated stories.
Believe in new stories that benefit you.

No one can make you discouraged unless you let them.
Refuse to give away your power to others.

당신이 허락하지 않는 한 그 누구도 당신을 주눅 들게 할 수 없습니다.
타인에게 당신의 권한을 주는 것을 거부하세요.

No one can make you discouraged unless you let them.
Refuse to give away your power to others.

In this world, there are brilliant people like you who
always use challenges to grow themselves.

이 세상엔 당신처럼 항상 도전을 통해 자신을 성장시키는 똑똑한 사람들이 있어요.

In this world, there are brilliant people like you who
always use challenges to grow themselves.

Energy

에너지

'에너지'와 관련된 나를 위한 긍정 메시지를 필기체로 써 보세요.

You are not broken. You are not lazy.
You have your own special set of superpowers.

당신은 망가지지 않습니다. 당신은 게으르지 않습니다.
당신은 자신만의 특별한 힘을 지닌 놀라운 존재입니다.

You are not broken. You are not lazy.
You have your own special set of superpowers.

The number one ingredient for high performance is
managing your energy level on a daily basis.

높은 성과를 내기 위해 가장 필요한 것은 자신의 에너지 수준을 매일 관리하는 것입니다.

The number one ingredient for high performance is
managing your energy level on a daily basis

If you are tired, don't just check on your body.
Check if your mind is rested, as well.

당신이 피곤하다면, 그저 몸만 확인하지 마세요.
당신의 마음이 쉬고 있는지도 확인해 보세요.

If you are tired, don't just check on your body.
Check if your mind is rested, as well.

Have you made your lifestyle easy for you to feel energetic? Or is it difficult?

당신의 라이프스타일은 에너지가 넘치는 것을 느끼기 쉽나요?
아니면 어려운가요?

Have you made your lifestyle easy for you to feel energetic? Or is it difficult?

Do you constantly listen to your inner critic that belittles you? That may be why your energy is low.

당신을 비하하는 당신의 내면의 비평에 끊임없이 귀를 기울이나요?
그것이 당신의 에너지가 낮은 이유일 수 있습니다.

Do you constantly listen to your inner critic that belittles you? That may be why your energy is low.

Sometimes simple habits are the key to higher energy.
Sleep well, exercise, and eat a healthy diet.

때때로 간단한 습관이 더 높은 에너지의 열쇠입니다.
숙면을 취하고, 운동을 하고, 건강한 식단을 먹는 것입니다.

Sometimes simple habits are the key to higher energy.
Sleep well, exercise, and eat a healthy diet.

Don't be so hard on yourself.
Give yourself enough space to recharge and heal.

스스로를 너무 힘들게 하지 마세요.
여러분 자신에게 재충전하고 치유할 수 있는 충분한 공간을 확보하세요.

Don't be so hard on yourself.
Give yourself enough space to recharge and heal.

Listen to things that will lift you up. Expose yourself to things that will remind you of your own strengths.

여러분의 기운을 돋우는 것들을 들으세요. 여러분 자신의 장점을 상기시킬 수 있는 것들에 여러분 자신을 노출시키세요.

Listen to things that will lift you up. Expose yourself
to things that will remind you of your own strengths.

If you stay hurt because of someone, you are choosing to give all your power away to that person.

만약 당신이 어떤 이 때문에 계속 상처받는다면, 그것은 당신의 모든 힘을 그 사람에게 넘겨주기로 선택하고 있는 것입니다.

If you stay hurt because of someone, you are choosing
to give all your power away to that person.

You must push through even when it feels like it
won't make any difference. Believe in yourself fiercely.

아무런 변화가 없을 것 같은 상황에서도 끝까지 밀고 나가야 합니다.
자신을 강하게 믿으세요.

You must push through even when it feels like it
won't make any difference. Believe in yourself fiercely

Even in quiet and rocky places, you are amazing and
powerful.

고요함 속에서도, 바위투성이의 장소에서도 당신은 놀랍고 강력합니다.

Even in quiet and rocky places, you are amazing and
powerful.

Your feelings drive your actions. Choose to feel focused, committed, confident, and certain.

당신의 감정이 당신의 행동을 움직입니다. 집중력, 헌신, 자신감, 확신을 가지도록 선택하세요.

Your feelings drive your actions. Choose to feel focused, committed, confident, and certain.

Nothing in this world can discourage you if you don't take things personally.

당신이 기분 나쁘게 받아들이지 않는다면 이 세상 무엇도 당신을 낙담시킬 수 없습니다.

Nothing in this world can discourage you if you don't take things personally.

Your problem is not a problem if you are determined to make your dreams a reality.

만약 여러분이 꿈을 현실로 만들기로 결심했다면, 여러분의 문제는 문제가 아닙니다.

Your problem is not a problem if you are determined to make your dreams a reality.

You can figure out anything in life.
Start telling truths about what you are capable of.

당신은 인생에서 무엇이든 해결할 수 있습니다.
여러분이 할 수 있는 것에 대해 진실을 말하기 시작하세요.

You can figure out anything in life.
Start telling truths about what you are capable of.

Time

시간

'시간'과 관련된 나를 위한 긍정 메시지를 필기체로 써 보세요.

Time is elastic. You can always stretch time for the things that matter to you.

시간은 유연합니다. 당신에게 중요한 것을 하기 위한 시간은 언제든 만들 수 있습니다.

Time is elastic. You can always stretch time for the things that matter to you.

Plan time to rest.

Schedule time to take care of yourself.

휴식을 계획하세요.

스스로를 돌볼 일정을 만드세요.

Plan time to rest.

Schedule time to take care of yourself.

If you don't rush through things but still live every day to the fullest, time is on your side.

일을 서두르지 않으면서 매일 최선을 다해 살고 있다면, 시간은 당신 편입니다.

If you don't rush through things but still live every

day to the fullest, time is on your side.

The main reason why we waste time is because of
unwanted feelings. We use time to escape from them.

우리가 시간을 낭비하는 주된 이유는 원치 않는 감정 때문입니다.
우리는 감정에서 벗어나기 위해 시간을 사용합니다.

The main reason why we waste time is because of
unwanted feelings. We use time to escape from them.

Manage your time by respecting the schedule you've
made for yourself. Practice honoring your plans.

당신이 스스로 만든 일정을 생각하면서 당신의 시간을 관리하세요.
자신의 계획을 존중하는 데 익숙해지세요.

Manage your time by respecting the schedule you've
made for yourself. Practice honoring your plans.

If you spend your time escaping from reality,
you can also use your time to change it.

당신이 현실로부터 도망치는 데 당신의 시간을 사용한다면, 당신은 그 현실을 바꾸는 데에도 당신의 시간을 사용할 수 있습니다.

If you spend your time escaping from reality,
you can also use your time to change it.

The secret to cherishing your relationships is to remind
yourself that you only have limited time with them.

관계를 소중히 여길 수 있는 비결은 그들과의 시간이 제한적이라는 것을 스스로에게 상기시키는 것입니다.

The secret to cherishing your relationships is to remind
yourself that you only have limited time with them.

When it comes to living your best day, it's not about
the quantity of time. It's about the quality.

최고의 하루를 살아가는 것은 시간의 양에 달려 있지 않습니다.
(시간의) 질에 달려 있습니다.

When it comes to living your best day, it's not about

the quantity of time. It's about the quality

We never know when our time is up.
Don't delay in living your dreams.

우리의 시간이 언제 끝나는지 알 수 없습니다.
꿈을 살아가는 것을 미루지 마세요

We never know when our time is up.

Don't delay in living your dreams.

There is not enough time to make excuses.
Decide what you truly want and do it.

변명을 할 시간이 없습니다.
당신이 무엇을 진정으로 원하는지 결정하고 그것을 하세요.

There is not enough time to make excuses.
Decide what you truly want and do it.

Make time for the things you love, because that's
what you deserve.

당신이 좋아하는 것을 하는 시간을 만드세요.
왜냐하면 당신은 그럴 자격이 있습니다.

Make time for the things you love, because that's
what you deserve.

Once you realize you can make time your ally, not
your enemy, you gain so much more control over it.

시간을 나의 적이 아닌 내 편으로 만들 수 있다는 것을 깨닫게 되면, 당신은 그것(시간)에 훨씬 주도권을 가질 수 있습니다.

Once you realize you can make time your ally, not
your enemy, you gain so much more control over it.

Life is too short to listen to the lies or negative
criticism from people who don't matter to you.

거짓말이나 당신에게 중요하지 않은 사람들의 부정적인 비난을 듣기엔 삶이 너무 짧습니다.

Life is too short to listen to the lies or negative
criticism from people who don't matter to you.

Don't say "yes" to everything. Don't please people at
the expense of your precious time.

모든 것에 "예"라고 말하지 마세요. 당신의 소중한 시간을 낭비하면서 사람들의 비위를 맞추지 마세요.

Don't say "yes" to everything. Don't please people at
the expense of your precious time.

People underestimate what they can do within a
decade. Be patient. You can do extraordinary things.

사람들은 10년 안에 그들이 할 수 있는 것을 과소평가합니다.
인내심을 가지세요. 여러분은 놀라운 일들을 할 수 있습니다.

People underestimate what they can do within a
decade. Be patient. You can do extraordinary things.

Decision

결정

'결정'과 관련된 나를 위한 긍정 메시지를 필기체로 써 보세요.

If you want to live a different life, you've got to make different decisions.

다른 삶을 살기 원한다면, 다른 결정을 내려야 합니다.

If you want to live a different life, you've got to make different decisions.

The more we make conscious decisions, the higher
chance we'll have to build the life we truly want.

의식적인 결정을 할수록 우리가 진정으로 원하는 삶을 건설할 가능성이 더 높아집니다.

The more we make conscious decisions, the higher
chance we'll have to build the life we truly want.

Indecision is also a decision. It's choosing to not feel
discomfort at the expense of your potential.

결정을 하지 못하는 것도 역시 결정입니다. 당신의 잠재력을 희생하면서 불편함을 느끼지 않는 것을 선택하는 것입니다.

Indecision is also a decision. It's choosing to not feel
discomfort at the expense of your potential.

Support your decisions by trusting yourself.
Have your own back when it comes to your choices.

여러분 자신을 신뢰함으로써 여러분의 결정을 지지하세요.
당신의 선택에 대해 당신만의 의견을 가지세요.

Support your decisions by trusting yourself.
Have your own back when it comes to your choices.

Try to avoid making decisions when your mind is full
of drama. Make a decision from a clean space.

여러분의 마음이 드라마틱할 때 결정을 내리는 것을 피하도록 노력하세요.
깨끗한 공간에서 결정을 내리세요.

Try to avoid making decisions when your mind is full
of drama. Make a decision from a clean space.

Sometimes making a decision doesn't feel so great.
It can be frightening. And that's okay.

때때로 결정을 내리는 것이 그렇게 좋지 않게 느껴집니다.
그것(결정을 내리는 것)은 무서울 수도 있습니다. 그래도 괜찮습니다.

Sometimes making a decision doesn't feel so great.
It can be frightening. And that's okay.

When things get tough, make a decision to gain better
skills and wisdom.

상황이 어려워질 때, 더 나은 기술과 지혜를 얻기 위한 결정을 내리세요.

When things get tough, make a decision to gain better
skills and wisdom.

Sometimes thinking deeply doesn't make it easier to make a decision. Thinking clearly does.

때때로 깊이 생각하는 것이 결정을 더 쉽게 만들지는 않습니다.
명확하게 생각하는 것이 그렇습니다. (결정을 더 쉽게 만듭니다.)

Sometimes thinking deeply doesn't make it easier to make a decision. Thinking clearly does.

Instead of doing nothing and worrying, come up with a strategy. Don't let anything stop you.

아무 일도 하지 않고 걱정만 하는 것 대신에 전략을 짜세요.
어떤 것도 당신을 막게 하지 마세요.

Instead of doing nothing and worrying, come up with a strategy. Don't let anything stop you.

Our results are created by our thoughts and actions,
not by a single decision.

우리의 결과는 우리의 생각과 행동에 의해 만들어집니다.
단 한 번의 결정으로 만들어지는 것이 아닙니다.

Our results are created by our thoughts and actions,
not by a single decision.

Don't make a decision out of fear. Make a decision
that is aligned with your values and desires.

두려움 때문에 결정을 내리지 마세요. 여러분의 가치관과 욕망에 맞는 결정을 내리세요.

Don't make a decision out of fear. Make a decision
that is aligned with your values and desires.

Taking action without making a decision may be the reason why you want to blame others for the results.

결심 없이 행동을 취하는 것은 결과에 대해 다른 사람들을 비난하고 싶기 때문일 수 있습니다.

Taking action without making a decision may be the

reason why you want to blame others for the results.

Believe that you already know the answers to your questions. It'll help you to tap into your wisdom.

자신의 질문에 이미 답을 갖고 있다고 믿으세요.
당신의 지혜를 발휘하는 데 도움이 될 겁니다.

Believe that you already know the answers to your

questions. It'll help you to tap into your wisdom.

Every thought is a choice. Every feeling is a choice.
You can choose differently.

모든 생각은 선택입니다. 모든 감정은 선택입니다.
선택을 다르게 하세요.

Every thought is a choice. Every feeling is a choice.
You can choose differently.

Your perspective changes your whole mood.
Your mood changes what you create in your reality.

당신의 관점은 당신의 전체 기분을 변화시킵니다.
여러분의 기분은 여러분이 현실에서 만들어 내는 것을 바꿉니다.

Your perspective changes your whole mood.
Your mood changes what you create in your reality.

Aliveness

생기

'생기'와 관련된 나를 위한 긍정 메시지를 필기체로 써 보세요.

Feeling bad is not a sign that there's something wrong with you. It's just part of living a human life.

기분이 나쁘다는 것은 여러분에게 문제가 있다는 것을 나타내는 징후가 아닙니다.
그것은 단지 인간 생활의 일부일 뿐입니다.

Feeling bad is not a sign that there's something wrong
with you. It's just part of living a human life.

Do you want to avoid negative emotions all the time
or do you want to fully experience your life?

당신은 항상 부정적인 감정을 피하고 싶나요, 아니면 당신의 삶을 완전히 경험하고 싶나요?

Do you want to avoid negative emotions all the time
or do you want to fully experience your life?

You are precious. Your life is priceless.
You get to be yourself only once in this life.

당신은 소중합니다. 당신의 삶은 값을 매길 수 없습니다.
당신은 이번 생에 단 한 번뿐인 당신 자신이 될 수 있습니다.

You are precious. Your life is priceless.
You get to be yourself only once in this life.

Connect with your people. Find people who share
the same interests as you and grow together.

사람들과 교류하세요. 당신과 같은 관심사를 공유하는 사람들을 찾아서 함께 성장해 보세요.

Connect with your people. Find people who share
the same interests as you and grow together.

Say yes to the challenge.
Say yes to new possibilities.

도전에 응하세요.
새로운 가능성에 응하세요.

Say yes to the challenge.
Say yes to new possibilities.

You are never "too old" or "too young" to go after what you are passionate about.

여러분은 결코 여러분이 열정을 가지고 있는 것을 추구하기에 나이가 너무 많거나 너무 어리지 않습니다.

You are never "too old" or "too young" to go after what you are passionate about.

Are you running away from something or running toward something? Do you like your answer?

당신은 무언가로부터 도망치고 있나요, 아니면 무언가를 향해 달리고 있나요?
당신의 대답이 마음에 드나요?

Are you running away from something or running toward something? Do you like your answer?

Feeling bored and frustrated is completely normal.
Let yourself feel bored and still move forward.

지루하고 좌절감을 느끼는 것은 완전히 정상입니다.
지루함을 느끼면서도 앞으로 나아가세요.

Feeling bored and frustrated is completely normal.
Let yourself feel bored and still move forward.

Do what matters to you. Go above and beyond
when it comes to what you're passionate about.

당신에게 중요한 일을 하세요. 여러분이 열정을 가지고 있는 것에 대해 그 이상을 추구하세요.

Do what matters to you. Go above and beyond
when it comes to what you're passionate about

If you're jealous, shift your focus.
Focus on your growth. Water your own garden.

만약 질투가 나면, 초점을 바꾸세요.
성장에 집중하세요. 자신의 정원에 물을 주세요.

If you're jealous, shift your focus.
Focus on your growth. Water your own garden.

You might feel ashamed when you step out of your
comfort zone. But it's worth it every single time.

여러분은 편안한 곳에서 나올 때 부끄러움을 느낄 수도 있습니다.
하지만 이것은 매번 가치가 있습니다.

You might feel ashamed when you step out of your
comfort zone. But it's worth it every single time.

People feel alive when they do things not because they have to, but because they genuinely want to.

사람들은 그들이 해야 하기 때문이 아니라, 그들이 진정으로 원하기 때문에 무언가를 할 때 살아 있음을 느낍니다.

People feel alive when they do things not because they have to, but because they genuinely want to.

Sadness, pain, and anxiety are not a part of you. They are feelings that come and go.

슬픔, 고통, 불안은 당신의 일부가 아닙니다.
그것들은 오고 가는 감정입니다.

Sadness, pain, and anxiety are not a part of you. They are feelings that come and go.

It's not greedy to desire many things.

It just means you are passionate.

많은 것을 욕망하는 것은 욕심이 아닙니다.
그것은 단지 여러분이 열정적이라는 것을 의미합니다.

It's not greedy to desire many things.

It just means you are passionate.

Don't settle for less than what you can be.

Strive for an extraordinary life.

당신이 될 수 있는 것보다 작은 것에 안주하지 마세요.
비범한 삶을 위해 노력하세요.

Don't settle for less than what you can be.

Strive for an extraordinary life.

Present

현재

'현재'와 관련된 나를 위한 긍정 메시지를 필기체로 써 보세요.

Let go of what has already happened, let the future unfold, and let yourself live in the present.

이미 일어난 일을 버리고, 미래가 펼쳐지도록 놔두고, 현재를 살아가십시오.

Let go of what has already happened, let the future unfold, and let yourself live in the present.

Regret is a choice. You can either constantly relive the past or you can gracefully move on.

후회하는 것은 선택입니다. 여러분은 끊임없이 과거를 회상하거나 품위 있게 나아갈 수 있습니다.

Regret is a choice. You can either constantly relive the past or you can gracefully move on.

If today were your last day, how would you live it differently?

오늘이 당신의 마지막 날이라면, 어떻게 다르게 살고 싶나요?

If today were your last day, how would you live it differently?

You can change your past by changing your present
interpretation of the past.

당신은 과거에 대한 현재의 해석을 바꿈으로써 과거를 바꿀 수 있습니다.

You can change your past by changing your present
interpretation of the past.

Take a moment to pause and breathe.
What do you want to remember today?

잠시 멈추고 숨을 쉬세요.
당신은 오늘 무엇을 기억하고 싶나요?

Take a moment to pause and breathe.
What do you want to remember today?

Forgive yourself for all your mistakes and move on.
You are still trustworthy and full of possibilities.

여러분의 모든 실수를 용서하고 앞으로 나아가세요.
당신은 여전히 신뢰할 수 있고, 가능성으로 가득 차 있습니다.

Forgive yourself for all your mistakes and move on.
You are still trustworthy and full of possibilities.

Instead of worrying about things that won't even
happen, love more, live more, and do more.

일어나지도 않은 일을 걱정하는 대신, 더 많이 사랑하고, 더 많이 살고, 더 많은 행동을 하세요.

Instead of worrying about things that won't even
happen, love more, live more, and do more.

Ask this question to check if your thought is helpful:
"is this thought current or is it outdated?"

당신의 생각이 도움이 되는지 확인하기 위해 이 질문을 하세요.
"이러한 생각은 현재 상태입니까, 아니면 시대에 뒤떨어진 것입니까?"

Ask this question to check if your thought is helpful:
"is this thought current or is it outdated?"

Take yourself off from autopilot and be conscious
of your thoughts, feelings, and actions.

무의식적으로 반복하는 일상에서 벗어나 여러분의 생각, 감정, 행동을 의식하세요.

Take yourself off from autopilot and be conscious
of your thoughts, feelings, and actions.

If you can be present with what you are feeling,
you can bond with yourself on a much deeper level.

만약 여러분이 느끼고 있는 어떤 것과도 함께 있을 수 있다면, 여러분은 훨씬 더 깊은 차원에서 여러분 자신과
유대감을 갖게 될 것입니다.

If you can be present with what you are feeling,
you can bond with yourself on a much deeper level.

Reinvent yourself, love yourself, discipline yourself,
and live each moment of your life wholeheartedly.

자신을 개발하고, 자신을 사랑하고, 자신을 단련하고, 여러분의 삶의 매 순간을 진심으로 사세요.

Reinvent yourself, love yourself, discipline yourself,
and live each moment of your life wholeheartedly.

Don't repeat the same old days and wonder why
you're not excited about your life.

예전과 같은 날들을 반복하지 말고 왜 여러분의 삶에 대해 흥분하지 않는지 궁금해하세요.

Don't repeat the same old days and wonder why
you're not excited about your life.

If you choose expansion, don't be surprised
when different challenges come up.

만약 여러분이 확장을 선택했다면, 다양한 어려움들이 다가와도 놀라지 마세요.

If you choose expansion, don't be surprised
when different challenges come up.

What makes life vibrant is living as your true self without any apologies or excuses.

삶을 활기차게 만드는 것은 어떠한 사과나 변명 없이 여러분의 진정한 모습으로 사는 것입니다.

What makes life vibrant is living as your true self without any apologies or excuses.

Be crystal clear about what you want.
No maybes or perhaps.

당신이 원하는 것을 확실히 하세요.
"아마도"나 "그럴지도"가 아니라요.

Be crystal clear about what you want.
No maybes or perhaps.

Love

‘사랑’과 관련된 나를 위한 긍정 메시지를 필기체로 써 보세요.

You are special. You are irreplaceable.
You can do amazing things.

당신은 특별해요. 당신은 대체할 수 없어요.
여러분은 놀라운 일들을 할 수 있습니다.

You are special. You are irreplaceable.
You can do amazing things.

If you loved yourself unconditionally, how would
your daily conversation with yourself be different?

자기 자신을 무조건적으로 사랑한다면, 자기 자신과의 대화는 얼마나 달라질까요?

If you loved yourself unconditionally, how would
your daily conversation with yourself be different?

There's so much more freedom in love than in hate.
No more energy is wasted.

사랑에는 증오보다 더 많은 자유가 있습니다.
더 이상 에너지를 낭비하지 않습니다.

There's so much more freedom in love than in hate.
No more energy is wasted.

Nothing is more powerful than having your own back. Live and create with that strong self-support.

자기 자신의 편이 되어 주는 것보다 더 강력한 것은 없습니다.
스스로 자신의 강력한 편이 되어 주며 삶을 살고 창조하세요.

*Nothing is more powerful than having your own
back. Live and create with that strong self-support.*

You can either believe people don't care about you or believe you are fully loved and supported.

여러분은 사람들이 여러분을 신경 쓰지 않는다고 믿거나 여러분이 완전히 사랑받고 지지받고 있다고 믿을 수 있습니다.

*You can either believe people don't care about you or
believe you are fully loved and supported.*

Loving isn't trying to fix something.
It is about being present and providing a safe space.

사랑하는 것은 무언가를 고치려고 노력하는 것이 아닙니다.
그것은 함께 있어 주고, 안전한 공간을 제공해 주는 것입니다.

Loving isn't trying to fix something.
It is about being present and providing a safe space.

Choosing love is beneficial. Choosing love will help you
feel love before anyone else.

사랑을 선택하는 것은 이롭습니다. 사랑을 선택하는 것은 여러분이 누구보다 먼저 사랑을 느낄 수 있도록 도
와줄 것입니다.

Choosing love is beneficial. Choosing love will help you
feel love before anyone else.

How can you have your own back today?

How can you appreciate yourself today?

오늘 어떻게 스스로의 편이 되어 줄 수 있나요?
오늘 어떻게 스스로에게 고마워할 수 있나요?

How can you have your own back today?

How can you appreciate yourself today?

Having your own back means deciding that you will be the solution to all your problems.

여러분의 지지를 받는다는 것은 여러분이 모든 문제에 대한 해결책이 될 것이라고 결정하는 것을 의미합니다.

Having your own back means deciding that you will be the solution to all your problems.

What if you could listen to yourself with grace
instead of judging yourself?

만약 여러분이 자신을 판단하는 대신 자상하게 자신의 말을 들을 수 있다면 어떨까요?

What if you could listen to yourself with grace
instead of judging yourself?

Be patient with yourself. Don't rush into anything
because you are already magnificent as you are.

자신에게 인내심을 가지세요. 당신은 이미 있는 그대로 훌륭하기 때문에 무슨 일이든 서두르지 마세요

Be patient with yourself. Don't rush into anything
because you are already magnificent as you are.

True love is not loving other people at the expense of losing yourself.

진정한 사랑은 자신을 잃는 대가로 다른 사람을 사랑하는 것이 아닙니다.

True love is not loving other people at the expense of losing yourself.

If you are not enough for you, no amount of recognition from others can satisfy you.

만약 당신이 당신에게 충분하지 않다면, 다른 사람들로부터 아무리 인정받아도 당신을 만족시킬 수 없습니다.

If you are not enough for you, no amount of recognition from others can satisfy you.

If someone is irritating you, check first if you've been
irritated by yourself.

만약 누군가가 당신을 짜증 나게 한다면, 먼저 당신 스스로에게 짜증이 나 있는지 확인하세요.

If someone is irritating you, check first if you've been
irritated by yourself.

If we are obsessed with controlling someone,
we lose our own power to control ourselves.

만약 우리가 누군가를 통제하는 것에 집착한다면, 우리는 우리 자신을 통제할 수 있는 힘을 잃게 됩니다.

If we are obsessed with controlling someone,
we lose our own power to control ourselves.

Authenticity

'진정성'과 관련된 나를 위한 긍정 메시지를 필기체로 써 보세요.

You are not born to fit in with the crowd.
You are born to stand out.

당신은 군중과 어울리도록 태어나지 않았습니다.
당신은 눈에 띄기 위해 태어났습니다.

You are not born to fit in with the crowd.
You are born to stand out.

The world doesn't need a perfect person.
What the world desperately needs is you.

세상은 완벽한 사람을 필요로 하지 않습니다.
세상이 절실히 필요로 하는 것은 당신입니다.

The world doesn't need a perfect person.
What the world desperately needs is you.

Your desires are sacred. They lead you to contribute
in a way that delights you.

당신의 욕망은 고귀합니다. 그것(당신의 욕망)들은 당신을 즐겁게 하는 방식으로 당신에게 기여하도록 이끕니다.

Your desires are sacred. They lead you to contribute
in a way that delights you.

If you can finally see how exceptional you are,
you don't need to compare or compete with others.

만약 여러분이 얼마나 뛰어난지 결국 알 수 있다면, 여러분은 비교하거나 경쟁할 필요가 없습니다.

If you can finally see how exceptional you are,
you don't need to compare or compete with others.

Being your true self is a form of contribution;
you inspire other people to be their authentic selves.

여러분의 진정한 모습이 되는 것은 기여의 한 형태입니다.
여러분은 다른 사람들 또한 진정한 자신이 되도록 영감을 줍니다.

Being your true self is a form of contribution;
you inspire other people to be their authentic selves.

Authenticity is liberating ourselves to create and love in a way that is aligned with who we really are.

진정성은 우리 자신이 자유롭게 우리의 진정한 모습과 일치하는 방법으로 창조하고 사랑할 수 있게 하는 것입니다.

Authenticity is liberating ourselves to create and love in a way that is aligned with who we really are.

Let go of who you think you should be, and let your true self be seen and heard.

여러분이 되어야 한다고 생각하는 것을 버리고, 여러분의 진정한 모습이 보이고 들리게 하세요.

Let go of who you think you should be, and let your true self be seen and heard.

People who judge are always going to judge either way.
So choosing to be you is always the better option.

판단하는 사람들은 언제나 어느 쪽이든 판단할 것입니다.
그렇기 때문에 당신다운 것을 선택하는 것이 언제나 더 나은 선택입니다.

People who judge are always going to judge either way.
So choosing to be you is always the better option.

Let people be amazed. Let people be disappointed.
Let yourself be unapologetically you.

사람들을 놀라게 하세요. 사람들이 실망하게 내버려 두세요.
미안한 기색도 없이 당신다워지세요.

Let people be amazed. Let people be disappointed.
Let yourself be unapologetically you.

Stay true to your values. Listen to your intuition and be free to be creative in your own way.

여러분의 가치관에 충실하세요. 여러분의 직관에 귀를 기울이고 여러분만의 방식으로 창의적일 수 있도록 하세요.

Stay true to your values. Listen to your intuition
and be free to be creative in your own way.

You don't have to play by other people's rules. Come up with your own definition of happiness and success.

당신은 다른 사람들의 규칙에 따를 필요 없습니다.
행복과 성공에 대한 자신만의 정의를 생각해 보세요.

You don't have to play by other people's rules. Come
up with your own definition of happiness and success.

No one has the perfect combination of your history, personality, and perspective.

어느 누구도 여러분의 역사, 성격, 그리고 관점의 완벽한 조합을 가지고 있지 않습니다.

No one has the perfect combination of your history, personality, and perspective.

If you are going to tell me about your weaknesses, be fair and talk about your strengths, too.

당신의 약점에 대해 이야기할 거라면, 공평하게 당신의 강점에 대해서도 이야기하세요.

If you are going to tell me about your weaknesses, be fair and talk about your strengths, too.

Owning who you are will empower you.
Own your worth, your beauty, and your strengths.

여러분이 누구인지 받아들이는 것은 여러분에게 힘을 줄 것입니다.
당신의 가치, 당신의 아름다움, 그리고 당신의 장점을 여러분의 것으로 받아들이세요.

Owning who you are will empower you.
Own your worth, your beauty, and your strengths.

Don't live up to the expectations of others.
Live to fulfill your own expectations.

다른 사람의 기대에 부응하지 마세요.
여러분 자신의 기대를 충족시키기 위해 살아 보세요.

Don't live up to the expectations of others.
Live to fulfill your own expectations.